Consider This

Charlotte Mason and the Classical Tradition

Study Guide

www.karenglass.net

ISBN-13: 978-1502844989

ISBN-10: 1502844982

Typeset using the Merriweather font family:
www.sorkintype.com

Book cover photo: Art Deco Tower, © Mlane | http://
www.dreamstime.com/ & http://www.stockfreeimages.com/

Using the study guide.

— ❦ —

Consider This: Charlotte Mason and the Classical Tradition can be read and thought about without the need for any additional study material. However, sometimes questions are useful for helping us focus our thoughts, and if you are using the book with a discussion group, these questions are a good place to start.

Although only a few questions are provided for each chapter, I tried very hard to make sure they are synthetic questions. If you aren't sure what I mean by that, I hope you will be by the time you finish reading the book.

I gathered quotes from many sources during the research phase of writing my book, and I'm happy that this study guide can provide a home for a few of the ones that were left out. In addition, I've suggested some additional topical reading for each chapter from Charlotte Mason's *Original Homeschooling Series*.

Charlotte Mason wrote, in the Preface to *Philosophy of Education*:

> The public good is our aim; and the methods proposed are applicable in any school. My object in offering this volume to the public is to urge upon all who are concerned with education a few salient principles which are generally either unknown or disregarded; and a few methods which like that bathing in Jordan, are too simple to commend themselves to the 'general.' Yet these principles and methods make education entirely effectual.

My purpose is much like hers. I believe, with Charlotte Mason, that a few salient principles and a few methods founded solidly upon them can make all the difference in the world. She was confident enough to assert that none of her statements rest "upon opinion only." She knew they worked because she had seen the results through more than thirty years of dedicated work with the Parents National Education Union. I have found her methods effective in my own home school, as have scores of other contemporary educators who have faithfully implemented her principles. I hope this study will make the truth of her principles a reality in your own educational efforts.

—Karen Glass

Nor am I so ignorant of the capacities of different ages as to think that we should straightway place a grievous burden upon tender minds and remorselessly exact close application. For one thing especially must be guarded against, lest one who cannot yet love studies come to hate them and even after the passing of childhood's years shrink from a bitter task once undergone.

—Quintilian

1 — Holding Hands with the Past

1. Charlotte Mason was thrust into a teaching responsibility with minimal preparation, but she took her job seriously and made educating herself a priority. What books about education have you read? Have you read any of the same authors Charlotte Mason read?

2. How would reading multiple perspectives from different historical eras contribute to making a person a better teacher today?

3. Is it possible to read only contemporary or recent authors and understand what education was like in the past? Why or why not?

Suggested reading: *Parents and Children*, p. 249–56

They knew how to go the readiest way to work; and seeing that science, when most rightly applied and best understood, can do no more but teach us prudence, moral honesty, and resolution, they thought fit, at first hand, to initiate their children with the knowledge of effects, and to instruct them, not by hearsay and rote, but by the experiment of action, in lively forming and moulding them; not only by words and precepts, but chiefly by works and examples; to the end it might not be a knowledge in the mind only, but its complexion and habit: not an acquisition, but a natural possession. One asking to this purpose, Agesilaus, what he thought most proper for boys to learn? "What they ought to do when they come to be men," said he.

—Montaigne

2 — A Little Lower Than the Angels

1. Why and how does the way we view a person affect our education philosophy? What does it mean when David Hicks says "No education is innocent of an attitude toward man and his purposes."

2. Can you think of any additional literary examples that subtly suggest hereditary determinism?

3. Charlotte Mason says that if we view children as undeveloped, incomplete beings, "we cannot do otherwise than despise children, however kindly and even tenderly we commit the offence." Can you think of any well-intentioned modern methods or ideas that actually disrespect children?

4. Charlotte Mason wrote her first two principles to make her view of man (or a child) clear to her contemporaries. Can you express your view of man in a sentence or two which would speak to our culture today? What cultural ideas might we need to refute in our principles?

Suggested reading: *Parents and Children*, p. 257–67

And although death be far off and a long life be assured, the formation of character should none the less begin early, because life must be spent not in learning but in acting.

—Comenius

3 — Actions Speak Louder

1. I once read a story about a family tradition. A young husband asked his new wife why she cut the end off of the ham before she cooked it, and she answered "because my mother did and her ham was delicious." So they inquired of her mother, who replied in turn, "that's what my mother always did." When they called grandma, she explained the reason for cutting the end off of the ham: "My pan is too small!" How might it be a mistake in education to imitate what classical educators were doing without understanding why they were doing it?

2. Does making character formation the ultimate goal of education mean that necessary skills can be neglected?

3. Do you agree with the classical premise that "right thinking leads to right action?" Could right thinking be a virtue without corresponding right action?

4. Right thinking does not begin with a list of rules that tell us "think this." How can right thinking be instilled a person?

Suggested reading: *Formation of Character*, p. 209–17

If any one should wish to deliberate why God prizes children so highly, he will find no weightier reason than this, that children are simpler and more susceptible to the remedy which the mercy of God grants to the lamentable condition of men. For this reason it is that Christ commands us elders to become as little children.

—Comenius

4 — Begins with a Single Step

1. Do you agree that humility is a necessary component to education? How does it help or hinder the learning process?

2. How is humility undermined in our educational practices?

3. Can you think of examples from literature or history in which humility, or the lack thereof, played a role in education?

4. Can you think of an occasion when you learned something from an unexpected source—maybe from a grumpy neighbor or a wise eight-year-old? Might we learn even more if we condition ourselves to expect to learn from everyone and everything we encounter?

Suggested reading: *Ourselves*, Book I, p. 126–30, and Book II, p.97–103 (Notice how many times the word *humble* appears.)

Without any predecessor to copy, Socrates fell as it were instinctively into that which Aristotle describes as the double tract of the dialectic process, breaking up the one into the many, and recombining the many into the one; though the latter or synthetical process he did not often perform himself, but strove to stimulate his hearer's mind so as to enable him to do it for himself.

—C.D. Yonge

5 — Finding the Forest amid the Trees

1. This chapter discusses one of the most important aspects of classical education. Taking the time to ponder synthetic thinking until you understand it is very important. Do you think your primary approach to knowledge is analytic or synthetic?

2. Augustine considered education to involve "ordering the affections." How is this similar to "education is the science of relations?" Do you think that Charlotte Mason made a "science" of relationships, or do you think she was using a popular catch-word to draw the attention of her readers to her point?

3. Often hobbies or interests are born in childhood that last throughout our lives. Can you think of a relationship you formed with any area of knowledge (geology, cooking, history, gardening, music) that has enriched your adult life? Do you lament missing out on forming a relationship with anything when you were younger?

4. It would be a mistake to think of synthetic thinking as "good" and analytic thinking as "bad." What relationship should ideally exist between synthetic thinking and analytic thinking?

Suggested reading: *Parents and Children*, p.268-79

Just as a living body increases in size without any straining or forcible extension of the limbs ; since if food, care, and exercise are properly supplied, the body grows and becomes strong, gradually, imperceptibly, and of its own accord. In the same way I maintain that nutriment, care, and exercise, prudently supplied to the mind, lead it naturally to wisdom, virtue, and piety.

—Comenius

6 — Drawing the Circle Closed

1. Can you describe the link between synthetic thinking and action? Do you agree that we are more motivated to act when our affections are involved?

2. If we focus our educational efforts on critical analysis, how might we hinder the growth of virtue?

3. This chapter says, "Classical education involves the heart as much as it does the mind." Can you explain how heart and mind should be linked in educational practices?

4. This chapter ties the ideas of the previous three chapters together. It is an attempt to synthesize several ideas into one by showing the links between them. If the pursuit of virtue, humility, and synthetic thinking do represent the classical ideal, might there be more than one way of realizing that ideal? Can we use this ideal to evaluate the validity of various educational practices?

Suggested reading: *Formation of Character*, **p. 401–18**

―――――――――――――――❦――――――――――――

The love of grammar and the advantages of reading are not confined to school days but last throughout a man's whole life.

―Quintilian

―――――――――――――――❦――――――――――――

7 — Then and Now

1. Could Quintilian have made his claim that "love of grammar" is not confined to school days buts "lasts throughout a man's whole life" if he had thought of grammar in modern terms?

2. Can you think of different educational practices that might be called classical that have been different in different times or places in history? When did schooling begin? What books were used?

3. Can you think of some reasons for learning Latin in the 21st century that don't resemble utilitarian reasons? How might learning Latin (or Greek) for those reasons change our teaching methods?

4. Chapter 7 says of human nature that "it is easier for us to follow the letter rather than the spirit of the law." What differences would there be between a classical education that "followed the letter" of the classical tradition and one that "followed the spirit"?

5. Is there any part of the classical tradition that has to be lost or sacrificed if we try to make it a universal education rather than one for the privileged few?

Suggested reading: *Formation of Character*, **p. 288-96**

Education is teaching our children to desire the right things.

—Plato

8 — Education Is...

1. How does creating a healthy educational environment serve the classical ideals of education? Can you think of any historical examples that illustrate an ideal learning environment?

2. How can discipline and atmosphere be balanced? Can too much or too little discipline hinder the ideal learning environment?

3. If you accept Charlotte Mason's assertion that the mind is a living thing that must be fed, does it affect how seriously we consider the creation of the proper diet? Can you think of physical dietary mistakes that might have educational equivalents? If we are feeding a mind, how will we measure our progress or success?

Suggested reading: *Philosophy of Education*, **p.94–111**

In the movements of the soul the most important wheel is the will; while the weights are the desires and affections which incline the will this way or that. The escapement is the reason, which measures and determines what, where, and how far anything should be sought after or avoided.

—Comenius

There are also valid processes of reasoning which lead to false conclusions...As, then, valid conclusions may be drawn not only from true but from false propositions, the laws of valid reasoning may easily be learnt in the schools, outside the pale of the Church. But the truth of propositions must be inquired into in the sacred books of the Church.

—Augustine

9 — Choose You This Day

1. Can you describe Charlotte Mason's guides to moral and intellectual self-management? What link exists between the way of the will and the way of reason?

2. The motto of the PNEU schools was "I am; I can; I ought; I will." Why does will come last in that list? How is the will important in the classical ideal?

3. Is it a part of human nature to depend too heavily on human reason? What makes reason such a powerful influence in our lives? Why does Charlotte Mason feel that it cannot be trusted?

4. This chapter includes a summary of the vital elements that make up the classical ideal. How might our efforts towards a classical education be hindered if we are missing one of them? If we pursue intellectual prowess over virtue? If we fail to remain humble? If we focus our efforts on critical thinking skills instead of synthetic ones?

Suggested reading: *Philosophy of Education*, **p. 128–153**

[Education] has virtue for her end, which is not, as the schoolmen say, situate upon the summit of a perpendicular, rugged, inaccessible precipice: such as have approached her find her, quite on the contrary, to be seated in a fair, fruitful, and flourishing plain, whence she easily discovers all things below; to which place any one may, however, arrive, if he know but the way, through shady, green, and sweetly-flourishing avenues, by a pleasant, easy, and smooth descent, like that of the celestial vault.

—Montaigne

10 — Just a Sliver

— ❦ —

1. Do you have a clear understanding of the words that surround classical education? University? Liberal Arts? Trivium? Grammar, Logic, and Rhetoric? Is your understanding informed by historical precedent and usage?

2. The use of the words "Trivium" and "Quadrivium" to refer to the seven liberal arts arose during the early medieval era, when Latin was still a widely spoken language. To the Romans, a trivium and a quadrivium were literally cross-roads. Why do you think those terms were chosen for the liberal arts? Do you think choosing those words was a reflection of their naturally synthetic thinking?

3. The development of synthetic thinking does require time. Do you think Charlotte Mason allowed too much or too little time when she suggested devoting fifteen years to synthetic learning? How can we make a program with that emphasis work in our contemporary environment which demands critical thinking and analysis at every level of education?

4. Do you think analytical thinking will be sharper and better if it is built upon a synthetic foundation? How long might it take to develop analytical skills in a young person who already has a synthetic relationship with knowledge? How long might it take an adult, educated to think in the analytic mode, to develop synthetic understanding?

Suggested reading: *Home Education*, **p.226–29 and** *School Education*, **p. 164–73**

I, unfortunate man that I am, am one of many thousands, who have miserably lost the sweetest spring-time of their whole life, and have wasted the fresh years of youth on scholastic trifles.

—Comenius

11 — In Which Charlotte Shows Us How

1. This chapter begins with Charlotte Mason's assertion that education is "no more than applied philosophy." What links are there between our philosophy of education and the practices we develop? What might an unclear or mixed philosophy look like when methods are developed?

2. Charlotte Mason tells us that a corollary principle of "education is the science of relations" is that no education is "worth the name" unless it it has made children at home in the world of books. Why are books at the center of classical education? Is there any other way to accomplish the classical ideal?

3. What difference is there between a synthetic study of science and an analytical one? Science is one subject that falls easily into analytical thinking if we are not careful. What can we do to make our approach to science more synthetic?

4. What is the role of a teacher in Charlotte Mason's vision of education? Can you think of historical or living examples of teachers who have fulfilled that role, at least in part?

5. Narration is the cornerstone of Charlotte Mason's methods and can take various forms. How does narration contribute to synthetic thinking?

Suggested reading: *School Education*, p. 148–63

And it is one of the distinctive features of good intellects not to love words, but the truth in words. For of what service is a golden key, if it cannot open what we want it to open?

—Augustine

12 — Rock Breaks Scissors

1. Can you figure out why this chapter is named "rock breaks scissors?" (Hint: What are scissors used for?) What is the rock?

2. Not everything labeled "postmodern" is bad, but the ideas behind postmodernism conflict with the ideals of classical education. Can you think of a book or movie that reflects postmodern ideas? Is there still something to learn from it?

3. Would it be possible or desirable to construct an educational program based on the classical ideal using only books published within the last one hundred years? Why or why not?

4. How will thinking synthetically set us apart from the postmodern culture around us? Is it possible for synthetic thinking to have an influence in that culture?

Suggested reading: *Philosophy of Education*, 313–327

The fear of the Lord is the beginning of Wisdom, and the knowledge of the holy is understanding

—*Proverbs 9:10*

Afterword

1. How does the classical model of learning about heroes to emulate mesh well with a Biblical perspective?

2. Is there a difference between the kind of humility that the Bible encourages and the kind of humility needed to be a lifelong learner? Is it possible to be humble in one area and not in another?

3. How would a synthetic approach to learning about the Bible differ from an analytical approach? Is there a role for analysis in Bible study as well?

4. Can you think of a Bible verse, story, or principle that illustrates synthetic thinking? How does the Bible show us that all knowledge is connected?

5. If the Biblical words "knowledge, understanding, and wisdom" are not equivalent to stages, what might we learn about education by examining the way those words are used in the Bible? Will it be compatible with classical education?

Suggested reading: *Parents and Children*, **p. 41–59**

Made in the USA
San Bernardino, CA
15 February 2018